Dark Poems of the

Inland Seas Region

by Bob Stevens

ISBN: 978-0-578-74947-1

eISBN: 978-0-578-74948-8

First Printing 2020

24 23 22 21 20   5 4 3 2 1

Dark Poems of the Inland Seas Region

by Bob Stevens

jrefund no. 2 (2020)

the kiss

the boneshade sickle bottom of the moon

poked a clean hole in the factory grey clouds

and there was a tiny glint of electricity

on the rusty springs of the screen door

as it crashed open and the lovers tumbled out

she pulled him by his necktie

through the clutter hazy gloom of that
backyard

her red dress a smolder in the funeral air

and her dark hair fell heavy in a curling
collapse

she dragged him on

his scuffle boot wine feet shuffled

the gore pump of his heart rocked a shuffle beat

as he said baby

and there was a tiny glint of electricity

from the cats perched on the alley fence

skinny rain wet gravel cats

with broken shock tails

perched like crows or poker players

studying everything

she leaned him against the fence

and let him dangle there at arm's length

running her tongue over her teeth

over her lipstick lips

cleaning her mouth for the attack

one of the cats

with half an ear and a long flat nose

started to whine a little siren

and the others slowly joined in

watching the girl

watching her hands find a grip in his belt loops

pulling her hips to smother his

nailing his ass to the fence with a creak of wood

and then

they kissed

at first all loose lips and then a thrust of tongue

a real wide-mouthed wrestle kiss

and the eyes of those cats started to glow green

as they watched

she grinded him hungry into the fence

until those cats started to sing

they wailed and began pacing, tails in a raised
ass twitch

a swipe and a hiss and a bristle back of
irritation

the heat started to boil them violent

and they wrestled and latched and mounted
each other

needle claws and barbed pricks ripping tender
flesh

the girl pulled his tie down and buttons
popped free

she pushed his head back

and started to bite and suck on his stubble neck

while his knees and feet struggled in a jerky
dance

the cats were tearing each other to ribbons

cackle howls and screeches in the red mangle

the moon dropped its sickle edge lower

and hot feline blood speckled those two

and decorated the kiss

comedown from the ages

she bought a pointed witch's hat at the costume
shop

and flashed her green peepers at the clerk

then she put the hat on and went home

her long black dress dragging through the
leaves

cats greeted her and imitated her sashay

into the kitchen

where, candles lit, she began working on her
last lover

once she'd cut his head off

and stuck it dripping in a high birdcage

above the snarl of feline fangs and claws

she unscrewed each of her fingers

and soaked them in some soapy water

her cats weaving through a maze of flicker

quick tails dodging the flames

over to sniff the dish of digits

they swam around in there like thick
watersnakes

and after they were clean

they started to slide out

long painted nails cautiously peering over the
rim

she placed her palms flat on the table

and one by one they crawled into place

humping a wet trail like rainy inchworms

and the shadows were growing outside like
shadows always grow

they swallow up the grass and grow

they swallow up the sidewalk and grow

until they cover the street still hungry

coiled greedy around the circles of lamppost
light

hidden in the leaves and pressed in bunches

those shadows create jagged roads

for the witch's cats to trot along and through

dead mice dangling like cigarettes

from tiny pointed smiles

haunted house of snow

the mighty upswing

of the gusty lake winds

frigid

heavy with departure

children sleeping

shivering cedar

the insomniac lighthouse

rigid blue tendons

of those deeper currents

groaning off the point

snow flying

getting deeper

hissing and swishing

while the mighty upswing

of the gusty lake winds

dunes the already fallen snow

into sculpted waves by billows and blows

look at them

as they wisp

and as they twirl

into vanishing sprays

spreading poltergeist fingers

in the late afternoon windowpane

where a woman sits alone

duct-taped album of pressed wildflowers

closed on her quiet lap

the spider web clock ticks

by the beer calendar

a tarnish clock

slowly

unwinding

and the temperature

well

it continues to drop

the obscured sun

sneaks away

declining before dinner

sleepytime

the woman blinks

her heart

starts

again

while a huddle of northern bobwhites

flinch and ruffle

thump and cuddle

up in the scarlet oak

and that brooding mother black bear

who sulked her way around the edge of the
property

all through the haze of late summer

with her prancing fly pestered cubs in tow

is now dreaming somewhere

back in the beyond

of buried birch and pine

dreaming of a treetop perch

and a stolen beekeeper screen of honey

gripped in shiny paws

maybe a basket of fat berries

dreaming

barely breathing

while all this blizzard whistles

the crusted freeze above her

and helen

seven months clean

left the snowshoes she borrowed

in the cigarette smoked pantry

she had quite a tale to tell

about a gliding night promenade

into the luminous desolation

of twilight in the buried woods

there are things out there

there must be

because the house of the sitting woman

breathes more than she does

because the mighty upswing

of the gusty lake winds

when the killer was baptized

big jesus

on his big cross

with nails and thorny crown

seemed to catch the infant's stare

and hold it wondrous

then the smiling priest handed the boy back to
his parents

he gagged and spit up on his mother's sunday
dress

and his little eyes flushed red for an instant

while outside someone was chasing a bird with
a broom

a bluster of wind pressing the stained glass
against the frames

little diaphanous doves, visible only to the
child

flew in and out of the vaulted ceiling

where painted saints gazed down

solemn and austere in their robes

then those doves darkened to grackles

to peck the chipping paint

and build nests in every halo

the lives of the saints

last night george was worried

worried that his rubbery legs

and the dizzy rye swoon of his head

would refuse him a safe walk home

he was tilting and weaving

drunk as a lord

picturing his little rented flat

a dump, really

but

it could seem quite heavenly

after last call

there was soup, cigars

blankets and a warm bed waiting

but old george was ferociously drunk

and he had a long walk ahead of him

the wind blew sandy snow over the deserted avenue

the dull streetlights trembled

all frozen

he was all alone

the dim lights and clinking glasses

and laughter and jokes of lucky's bar

were far behind him now

nothing but a gusty whistle of bonechill winds

and the plod and crunch of his footfalls

the labored wheeze of his nicotine throat

and the round glowing bulb of his red nose

across the tundra of the west side he struggled

detecting no real signs of life

most of the houses he passed were dark

responsible citizens behind those doors

he thought ruefully

with their children tucked in

and their alarms set for an early rise

all their nice expensive things arranged just so

nice furniture, nice stereo, nice everything

it was tempting

george could understand why people became
thieves

but he decided he was too damn old

and it was too damn cold

to start a life of crime now

plus he just wasn't the type

never was

never would be

he was the giving type

the problem was that he gave too much

gave until he had nothing left for himself

for this reason, among others

he was a celebrated regular at lucky's

he proved that even a lush of no means

could be generous

his goodness was poor insulation, though

and the subzero wind blew down his throat

choking him, stealing his breath

he was starting to get scared

thinking about all that whiskey in his blood

and the cold windy subzero blackness that
surrounded him

and what happened to the widow maggie

during the holidays last year

poor old winehead maggie, george sighed

just two blocks from the bar

just another three blocks to her house

and she made the fatal decision to take a rest

hypothermia got her

all alone, in the dark

george shivered

just keep movin', just get home

glassy eyed in the icy breeze he forged ahead

concentrating on a tricky sidewalk

that weaved like a grey snake in front of him

he fell once

nearly crowning himself

on a snow-capped fire hydrant

this is dangerous, he proclaimed out loud

but i am in control

then he saw something to his right

the collapsed remains of a snowman perhaps

he turned to look and stared in disbelief

no, can't be

but it was

it was maggie

blue skinned and covered in snow

an icicle stretched off her nose

black lips and white eyes with her scarf flapping

she smiled then vanished in a blur of blown whiteness

george rubbed his eyes with his gloves

spirits from the bottle, that's all

his breath pumped out like factory smoke

using the fire hydrant

as a crutch to get back to his feet

he was saying oh jesus

i'll never make it home tonight, it's too far

you should know better, you old fool

he trudged forward

certain he was already frostbitten

close to collapsing for good

and then he remembered st. anthony's

just around the corner

he could see the tall sturdy beacon

of its yellow light green copper steeple

he could make out the gargoyles up there

hunched and catching snowflakes on their grey
tongues

they can't refuse me

i was baptized there and besides

church doors ain't never supposed to be locked

he blinked stars of new hope, that's what they say

i can go there and fall on the nod awhile

get my energies back

he stumbled on, leaving the ghost of maggie behind

and was crossing the street when a cop car
rolled by

the first car he'd seen

george smiled with all his missing teeth

and waved

the cop shook his crewcut blockhead

didn't wave back and drove on

when he turned a corner and was out of sight

george struggled up those freshly salted church
steps

and tried the doors

they were locked

he yanked harder, desperately

please, come on, i'm a goddamn catholic

in red faced spitting frustration

he kicked the door with his heavy galoshes

it popped open

he looked around

cautiously

feeling like an intruder

the streets were still empty

the houses were still dark

he slipped inside

shutting the big creaky wooden door behind
him

through the vestibule he stepped lightly

the church hadn't changed much in thirty years

it was as majestic and ornate as ever

the air hanging thick with dust

and incense and mystery and wedding rings
and caskets

the painted cathedral ceilings, the massive
chandelier

towering pipe organ silent in the balcony

so many eyes seemed to be watching him

the almond shaped painted eyes of the icons

the finely carved statue eyes of the angels

and the imploring eyes of a bloody tortured jesus

hanging emaciated on the twelve-foot altar
crucifix

george waved to him just as he'd waved to the cop

jesus didn't wave back either

but george understood

the lord had an excuse

poor jesus, he whispered

then cleared his throat

the hack echoed back and forth

bouncing around the vaulted heights

so quiet and spacious and

all those austere holy eyes

were still watching him

as he wiped his nose on his coat sleeve

and dipped his hand in the holy water font

making a teetering sign of the cross

he solemnly removed his hat and held it

with both hands crossed at his waist

head down in respect

he navigated to the last pew

crawled in

pulled off his coat

molded it into a pillow

laid his head down on it

and quickly

and deeply

he fell asleep

it wasn't long

before he had a dream

the thick liquid drapery of his mind

pulled apart and blue smoke departed

and there he was with a light snow falling

back in front of lucky's bar

the neon sign was buzzing open

still open

george automatically checked his wallet

his cheeks glowed with a radiant smile

when he found two twenties and a five

that's enough for me and ed, too

hopefully he ain't left yet

feeling like royalty, he lifted his whisker chin

and pushed through the familiar doors

and then, once inside

he stopped cold

ed wasn't in there

matter of fact, no one he knew was there

even the bartender was different

some young guy with a bashed up face

looked like a fighter

who never blocked a punch

george figured he'd get a drink anyway

he took the shortest route to the nearest stool

and sat down

there were a dozen or so bodies scattered around

and george surveyed the scene with growing

confusion

frightening faces

he saw women dressed like nuns

men in long brown hooded monk robes

a young girl, maybe twelve, sitting at the bar

strikingly beautiful and wearing a white dress

the bartender came over

circled a rag over the bartop in front of george

and spoke with a garbled lisp

can I help you, sir?

george nodded and asked for a beer

when the strange bartender came back

george grabbed his sleeve

hold it, buddy, who the hell are you?

what happened to this place?

where's craig and fran and ed, huh?

the bartender smiled through his broken face

he was missing his front teeth

i'm st. stephen, he said

george took a drink of beer

eyeballing the ugly barkeep over his glass

he swallowed, wiped his mouth

three empty stools down from him

next to the pretty girl in white

sat a young woman

she had long, beautiful hair that concealed her face

george noticed a cracked blue dish in front of her

he strained to get a better look and he gagged

there were two eyeballs resting there

like small wet eggs in a porcelain nest

the woman swept her long hair away

and looked at george with black empty sockets

george leapt back

yikes

then reached out and grabbed the bartender by
his shirt

what the hell kinda freak show you runnin' in here

st. stephen smiled warmly

don't be afraid of her, my friend

that's st. lucy, you remember the story

she's the sicilian virgin martyr

ripped her own eyes out, she did

to keep the men from buggin' her

the young girl in the white dress next to her is
st. agnes

poor thing is only thirteen, drinks like a fish

the bartender lowered his voice

but I never cut her off, after all

she's the patron saint of young virgins

lucy and agnes always come in here together

they have a lot in common

neither of 'em ever got laid and

both were martyred in the diocletion
persecution

the fella next to agnes, the bartender pointed

the one with the arrows stuck in him?

that's st. sebastian, I know you remember him

you wrote a report on him

in catechism when you were nine

remember?

george did remember

and slowly loosened his grip on the bartender

with jaw dropped he looked around

everyone in lucky's was a catholic saint

none looked very happy

st. jerome was all by himself at the far end of
the bar

slumped forward passed out and drooling on a
stack of papers

st. appolonia, wearing a necklace of her own teeth

was knocking back gin with st. catherine of siena

catherine was looking into thin air terrified

having visions of dancing well hung demons

chain-fucking with sharp tooth grins

wheeling through the smoky air

she mumbled, groaned, downed a shot and hid
her face

george heard maniac laughter and looked up

a strange woman in rags

with wild grey hair and gnarled hands

was hanging from the chandelier

which was swaying and cracking the plaster

she was spitting white in the dirty golden light

a frothy gob landed on george's shoulder

she bellowed with infernal satisfaction

as he wiped the mess away in disgust

the bartender leaned in and whispered

you know who that is?

that's st. christina, born in belgium back in 1150

she's real unpredictable, she bit me once

she's the one that jumped out of her coffin

during the middle of her requiem mass

and then flew up to the rafters of the church

st. stephen shrugged, she doesn't even drink

I guess she just likes that chandelier

but be careful, my friend

if you walk underneath her

she'll try to crap on you like a bird

george looked up at the wild woman

who pulled dry lips away from rotten teeth

in a terrifying grimace

flicking her tongue in and out

sick, george said, turning away

all these people are sad

and very fucking sick

you sure they're all saints?

stephen nodded

all saints, my friend

all saints

his voice echoed

and a glowing nimbus formed around his head

he touched george's glass with a gentle finger

it filled back to the brim with beer

a bruise of inky fog swept through the room

and the entire bar started to darken and fade

as george lifted the glass to drink

he heard st. stephen's voice in the thickening
shadows

we're all saints here

including you, george

we're all saints here

we're always here

everything went black

everything went silent

george opened his eyes

the dream was gone

he was once again

in the immaculate

silence

of the church

curled up in the back pew

he thought he could hear a retreating echo

of his drunken snoring

and felt embarrassed

but his bones were warm again

he could make it home now

he stood up and stretched

made the sign of the cross

thanked christ

and went back into the frozen night

no longer afraid

the thieving flood

the thieving flood came

in the last week of march

given a swollen birth by cracking ice floe thaw

and brooding grey cloud cover

filled with endless silver rain

the thieving flood rose slowly

climbing the riverside cattails

pruning the collected bare forest of
unnecessary stems

lifting a mulch of frosty dead leaves to float
from the steeper banks

dancing those shrinking ice wedges in
dissolving pirouettes

the thieving flood

rose

invigorated by the spells of malevolent witches

splashed by the ongoing rain that turned to
sleet by darkness

pushed from below where groggy fish swam
into one another

elevated to levels nervously reported on the
evening news

the need to think of sandbags

the clearing of basements and lower floors

the damn choking ice in the muddy throat of
the river

the thieving flood

there were a lot of phone calls amongst the
riverside folks

mary ann duly reported the expected
disappearance of her dock

there was a camera crew testing their lights at
the end of chippewa street

there were gathering congregations at the
hardware and grocery stores

shivering men in woolrich jackets waited

under dripping overhangs for bars to open

they needed the whiskey camaraderie to face
their seasonal foe

the thieving flood

the thieving flood that continued to rise

climbing over the slopes of dead grass yards

pooling the corded bulges of willow trunks

lifting the solemn drapery of their drooping
branches

it rose

invigorated by the growing mass of all it
absconded

splashed by the endeavors of defiant citizens in
waders and boots

pooled now around the stop sign by the boat
dock at the end of chippewa

elevated on the airwaves to the level of fucking
calamity

the worst flood in this river basin since the
flood of fifty-four

the flood of fifty-four that carried away both
bridge and livestock

the flood of fifty-four that announced itself

with clipping winds so strong that they rang
the church bells

and blew out the front window of the general store

killing larry wilkins with an arrowhead chunk
of glass to the jugular

spouting red onto the rack of field and stream
magazines

this was a lethal overflow

there were boat rescues of the elderly and
stubborn

who shared in common their requests for alcohol

there was a break in the weather

and the sun came on blinding

but the thieving river still rose

and it easily conquered those dead marshes

pressing the reeds slantwise before swallowing
them whole

rushing into the long meadow that leads to the
lawson place

taking down a section of rotting fence and
carrying the soggy bits

up across linda's hibernating vegetable garden

and right through her rosebush thicket

and she said one rosary after another with the
radio on

and her phone kept ringing as her back porch
was breached

a busted portion of her fence nudging itself up
each step in the icy froth

so she slid her beads into the folded protection
of her dusty skirt

then climbed the ladder to the attic with a fifth
of vodka

to join the blankets and photo albums

she had huffed up the night before

and soon her kitchen rug

lifted from the floorboards

and the water kept coming

as the thieving flood rose

buzzed by helicopters

up the road the situation was worse

daniel sorrel was sitting on his roof

dreary in the grey mist and smoking a cigarette

with his ruddy face of lug nut ears and ice
hockey scars

beer piss warming his pant leg

the blue jay perched in the drooping elm tree
branches above

could hear dan unspooling a drool of gibberish
to himself

as he checked the oily chambers of his revolver

and then that belligerent bird flew away

when dan fired one shot after another

into the determined and darkening floodwaters

and in the elkhart house there was a worried
husband

who knew that his shallow graves near the

edge of the woods

were now being covered by a sliding swirl

and those garbage bags of prostitute bones

were loosening

there was nothing he could do now

but boil more tea water

and hope that the little red devils who guided him

ligature by ligature with his truck in park

were now out there stamping down those

ballooning bags

but there was no sign of diabolical intervention

just the ever-encroaching tidal elevation

and the gathering clouds of further rainfall

and in the center of town

in the back room of the carla and son's bakery

there were sounds of shouting and slapping flesh

carla had her sparrow brown tresses all undone

and was braced skirt up against her
grandmothers cast iron stove

getting serviced by the syncopated pounding
thrusts

of jaw-clenched and dimple-chinned gary the
policeman

who was still in uniform from the waist up

hat and all

and by the time he came with a shout of
fucking christ

the rising waters had turned the higher ground
on the lindell peninsula

into an ever-shrinking island where a dozen
empty houses shuddered

families from those abodes convened and
claustrophobic

in the union hall on catalpa

youngsters bitching about the lack of internet access

while outside the thieving flood rose even more

and it carried off the fish found dead not sleeping

and it carried off an uprooted mailbox that
wheeled like a compass

and it carried off tapioca flecks of woodpile bark

and it rose and continued to rise

and it carried off three shivering calico kittens
in a soup kettle

and it carried off the drooping corpses of the
henderson fowl

and it carried off the contents of a forgotten
tackle box

bobbers and hooks and long undulations of
fishing line

and it rose and continued to rise

and it carried off stale candy hearts

dissolving them in slow motion powder explosions

and it carried off the same old lines off the

same old page

books pulled from their shelves

by a tide muscling through broken windows

and it carried off the mallard duck print curtains

moving them like silent flicker phantoms

the glacial pace transformed

and it carried off those who could not sleep

just as it carried off those

who could no longer stay awake

and it rose and rose

and it snatched away the rooftops

and all was lost

to the greedy thieving flood

inamorata

last night caught me dreaming

dreaming of a woman

a blood secret companion

who moves in a suspiria

down along some grey river

pale hands hoisting a batwing umbrella

rainy birds following her

she moves quietly

her dress soaked by her april stroll

rustling like the overwash of drainpipes

rain down the smoking chimney

on the slanty roof of her little home

my dream follows her

up a winding tree creaking street

hears her humming softly

a song about a reverie

a song about pretending there's a moon

she moves in that sensual misty

the details of her appearance always shifting

like the sink of fallen petals in a pond

transfigured by breezes

and obscured by twirling leaves

into various forms of breathtaking

the dream never allows me many details

i've had this dream many times

but last night

as she made it up on her porch

I could see her hoop earrings clearly

a glint as she shook out her umbrella

and dug around for her keys

and the blood red of her lips

the lovely creases at her eyes

evidence of some miles and motels

some all-nighter's and some drugs and wine

creased from squinting through freeze and
smoke

and ready for warmer evenings

on the edge, almost, of sparkling

those eyes on fire like

lanterns of jack

the eyes that will melt my bones

when she opens that door and takes me

into the strange haunt that is her world

a place of kettles and whiskey and twine

and hot tea and roots and viola

she will breathe fire

swallow swords and terrify small children

dogs barking as she poisons her apples

humming another song

she is always humming

always the most melancholy melody

as the shadows move through her house

like bulging snakes over the walls

and down into restless piles beneath her bed

as she stretches to yawn at four in the morning

when she crosses her legs shy spirits blush

and when the wolfbane blooms

and her smile

rarely surrendered in full

emerges glorious

like a full moon from a cloud bank

she'll have a place for my muddy shoes

and a rolled up blanket for my muddy head

and four wonderful words

make yourself at home

the cat lady

last night the cat lady stared at the ceiling

her mouth open slightly and shiny with blood

her throat a sparkling windpipe gash

from ear to ear

dust from the flourish of murder

still drifting the dim air

a shadow of the intruder, it seems

left in the creases of the burgundy curtains

that stirred over the jagged shatters

of windowpane on the floor

but he was gone

sipping from a bottle on the far side of town

studying his new collection of pearl necklaces

he was gone and there was only a single tiffany lamp

to orange light the quiet scene he left behind

embroideries and throw rugs

and dusty antiques

an old wooden icebox full of photo albums

dried flower petals in a bowl sniffed by one of her cats

another cat was sleeping peaceful, head on front paws

in the old woman's fireplace rocking chair

another wandered with early summer languid sways around the room

and a third, a fat bellied tabby, sat on the corpse's chest

lapping a lazy tongue on bloody paws, purring slightly

two other cats leapt out the broken window to
chase the night

hiding from the moonlight with excited
pounces into tree shadows

the breeze so warm and full of promise

banks of the ecorse

the snail-paced muddy floes of the ecorse creek

that gumbo of murky water we followed as kids

traipsing

sticks and bottles in hand

down the banks, where, when the water receded

you'd find all types of things

fender bender crunched car doors rusting

shopping carts draped in slimy green braids

bowling bags filled with tadpoles

and, at least once, a rotting corpse

most likely not the first or last one down here

it wasn't a homicide, though

here's the scene

they found the clumsy remains of a whiskey-
soaked stick boy

cops had to fight back the midsummer crowds

even an ice cream truck smelled the blood and
stopped

made a lotta money

everyone millin' around, suckin' on push-ups
and bomb pops

while they dragged the body

up the slippery banks

boots sliding in bottle caps and broken glass

one, two, three and a big hoist nearly tore the
arm off

it made a sick cracking sound and the crowd
seemed thrilled

the lead officer looked back over his shoulder

at first apologetically

and then angrily

get these damn people back,

nobody needs to see this

the three young officers designated to crowd control

snapped awake and put on their tough faces

you heard him, they said, step back

then the lead officer went to work on the grisly
task by himself

the dead man was rested on the bank

feet in the water, arms over his head

a reclining skeleton stinking up the breeze

his shirt started to quiver and flap

a carp had gotten under his collar

and was trapped by the buttons

the lead officer audibly gulped and attempted

to set the fish free

leaning over the body, his feet slipped and he fell

humped on the corpse in horror

both figures glided back into the creek

the fish wiggling frantically in the press of their
embrace

the paramedics, who had been standing at a
safe distance

through the whole episode

threw down their cigarettes and went in to help

the lead officer stumbled back into view- a
mess

he'd lost his morning coffee and doughnuts in
a splash

down the front of his uniform

this is the little polluted ribbon of water I
remember

it ran through my parent's backyard

the campfire

last night near the great thick flow of the
salteaux river

that pressed century old broken lumberman
bones to sand

eleven year old eddie

freckled and awkward and shy

trembled by the campfire, poking a twig
nervously in the flames

he trembled to his grandmother's words

to her tales of cold northern ghosts

wandering lighthouse shorelines with lanterns,
still in love

mourning on forgotten graves under the windy
lean of thick pines

and there across suffocating fields of ragweed
and goldenrod

waxy fingers of blue light curling from rotted
woodsheds

eddie shivered

the throbbing sun and its warmth had fallen

living bright olive green darkened to deep
emerald shadows

and the night monsters had taken flight

the only way night monsters can

crooked and hungry by whistling starlight

across the blackened fish heavy lake

over wet wilds in their menacing hush drone of
swoops

sending all good children to bed

eleven year old eddie was among the slumber
bound

his grandmother's warnings flapping like

sticky wings in his brain

but

it was

part of summertime

it was

the fresh chill of expectant wonder

of feral possibilities

it was

seven days away

in the northern woods

it was storytime

it was memorytime

it was a wondrous departure for little eddie

away from the evil faced shit smelling bullies at
school

away from the factory air and crowded houses
of home

away

into the green embrace of overgrown dirt trails

welcomed by the rolling echo and chime
chorus of birds

their chatter spread for miles and miles and

clean chill lakewater air sunburns

deep woods repellent

carrying the perch bucket and poles for
grandma at sunrise

collecting blueberries in a bucket at hazy
midday

listening to her stories at sunset

in front of a musty mosquito net flap and

crooked pole tent

sloping off a rusty weed cushioned trailer

there by the campfire

with words she unscrewed the soft top of

eddies skull

and sprinkled the luminescent red purple

powder of dreams

directly into the pink sponge of his

unsuspecting brain

crickety distant bellow from far on the lake

crickety distant bellow from afar

his slavic red faced immigrant grandmother, suddenly

suddenly

curved a finger his way

eddie, did you hear that?

She looked up over the sway of evening trees,
hunch backed

slack-jawed and wonder eyed

oh, the owl, he giggled uneasy, that's just an
owl

no, eddie, out over the lake, listen, oh my,
that's them

it was the way she said

them

that made eddie whisper

that's who?

oh my, oh my, little boys should be in bed

what, grandma? He asked anxiously, half
excited, half terrified

I didn't realize how late it is, ten o'clock, my my,

that is the usual time for them to rise and
crickety bellow

what, grandma, what, tell me, please

her eyes sparkled

with orange light

as a firefly cloud of ashes crackled

from the flames on a dangerous gusty rise

to the branches of a yellow birch overhead

crack and sizzle

a twig snaps

she considered, fat fingers rolling a loose chin

I suppose there is time to tell you a bit

and you're old enough that you should know

but I hafta be quick

time is short

the moon is cooling the air for strange things

but eddie, listen carefully

in the middle of the lake- out there

though you can't see it from shore- is an island

or what's left of it

used to be that people lived out there

but they all left and died years ago

taking their secrets to the worms

now I guess it's mostly marsh and reeds and
mossy trees

sometimes you can see a toppled tin roof,
swallowed by vines

or maybe a tireswing ripple kissing the water
on a tattered rope

your grandfather and I used to fish out there

find a shady spot, anchor down

he drove me crazy with his whistling

the most superstitious man

the most lovely man, god rest his soul

he whistled the entire time we were out there,
knees shakin'

but we only went there during the day, of course

at night it ain't safe

if you held a crucifix in your hands

near that sunken place at sunset

your fingers would burn

the evil there is heavy

even though there are some good fishin' spots

it's not recommended that anyone ventures near

that's a bewitched place, eddie, don't know
how or why

but it's wrong in the afternoon

and deadly by night, even for grown ups

for children it's worse because

well

oh, eddie

that's where

that's where the goony birds live

eddie gulped, the

goony birds

yes, the goony birds

and they eat little children, they love to eat little
children

with a curling strength of monster claws they'll
grab a child

and with a crickety bellow back across the
glassy black waters

to their swampy nests in the dead roots and
tadpoles

nests of twigs and bones that look like a
beaver's dam

in through a ragged hole they'll take you

never from that ragged hole will you emerge

that's why you hafta get back in the trailer
soon, my dear eddie

climb into your bunk and get under those
indian blankets

you'll be safe in there

as for me, i'll be alright out here on my own

what would those goony birds want with an
old lady and her vodka

but you, your bedtime is now for a good reason

you better get

I can hear 'em startin' to flap their foul wings
out there

listen

grandma

yes

what do they look like?

oh, eddie, I hope you never live to see one

i've seen them a few times

ugly damn birds, pardon my french, hideous to
the eye

let me tell you this

i've never seen or heard of bigger birds in all
my days

ten-foot wingspans of wild thick black brown
feathers

clingy with the swampy stink of mud and algae

still wet by starshine and sparkling like
bloodbaths

they glide along like quietly buzzing midnight
air raids

an occasional heavy thunder flap of wings

but mostly they glide

exchanging throaty calls back and forth

that sound like a cat purr rippling in saliva

a frightening sound, a sound that always ices
my back

oh eddie, and their faces

she made the sign of the cross and kissed her
crucifix

their faces make me think that maybe once they
were human

maybe the poor souls that used to live on that island

so animated, so sinister, so much like people

they have round bald heads as big as a fat
man's belly

perched on long naked droopy buzzard necks

and their bulging eyes are always rollin' back
and forth

their eyes are the most terrible part

bloodshot crazy and sparkling with hunger

always watching for those bad children not
tucked away

the stubborn ones who refuse to say their
bedtime prayers

they fly all night with grumbling stomachs

ravenous red tongues flopping from their hawk
sharp beaks

and when they grab a child they do it with
their claws

by the seat of their pants so they dangle
headfirst

screaming as the goony birds take them higher
and higher

before plummeting down through the whip of
cold lake air

to enjoy the tender catch in their grendel dens

they eat everything but the bones

which they use to strengthen

the twig and muck tapestry of the walls

when they can't find children, well

they've been known to carry off livestock,
especially pigs

farmers find splashes of blood in the angry dawn

a few pigs gone, and they hate the goony birds
in a fierce way

but none would actually row to the island for
revenge

brave fools who made the attempt didn't even
leave bones behind

you see, eddie, the goony birds are not alone
out there

they have a mother

eddie started to chew on his fingernails

a mother? the goony birds?

Yes, even goony birds hafta have a mother

but, I can't tell you about her, not now, sweet
child

it's already gotten so late, they'll be here any
second

crickety distant bellow

listen

please grandma, tell me

what does the mother of the goony birds look like?

now grandma tried to make it a point

to never drink in front of young eddie, it wasn't
proper

but she was thirsty and impatient

she took her stoli pint from the inside pocket of
her jacket

and wagged it around her face to clear the busy

mosquitoes away

then she uncapped it

shaking her head with a pout of wrinkled lips

eddie, eddie, eddie

i'll tell you what she looks like if you promise me

that when I say run- you run inside and dive
into bed, o.k.?

i'll hear them coming before you

so promise

eddie promised

grandma took a drink

the familiar tasty scorch made her grin, teeth
pressed together

the mother of the goony birds is a real bitch

pardon my french, and she's twice as big as her
offspring

her shadow in flight would darken our entire
campsite

and she... oh eddie

oh no

run

run, you heard me, run

her face twisted into a grimace of fear eddie
had never seen

and inky whooshes of gargantuan flaps

shook the frightened treetops like hissing
stormwinds

he imagined his hair standing on end and then

he ran through the tent in a blur, into the trailer and

vaulted himself safely and acrobatically on his
bunk bed

heart heaving into his ribcage, blankets hoisted
over his eyes

almost, he panted

they almost got me

fear subsided blueshade into exhaustion

and then melted nightshade into sleep

the deep wondrous sleep of northern
midsummer

outside grandma restrained her laughter as
best she could

and drank in meditative tips from her shiny bottle

the fire nothing more than shimmering coals

the vodka making her sigh in childhood
remembrance

the forest was immaculate and wordless

the forest was still

an hour later

eddie awoke

and threw his patchwork covers away to the sound of a storm

and someone shouting hysterical out in the windy chaos

the entire trailer heaved and was beaten by snapping branches

he recognized the shouts

it was grandma and she was in trouble

eddie slid down the bunk ladder

and skidded in his socks to the pollen dusted windows

what he saw left him open mouthed and breathless with fright

grandma was swinging a shovel in the air

fending off two giant churning goony birds

one was clutching a tattered bloody pig and snapping at grandma

the other was trying to grab something from
the dirt

grandma connected with a clang to its bald head

but then lost the shovel when it reared up and
screeched

it swept its long neck back down and snagged
what it came for

her vodka bottle

and then the two monsters lifted away like a
nightmare

dead pig and liquor in tow

grandma's hair was wild as she stood

legs apart

shaking her fist skyward

in the still buzzing night air

natural death

last night, as dusk fell, an excited faye tried to relax

smoking a menthol cigarette between pencil thin fingers

on the back porch of her little binding cabin in the woods

slowly creaking with a stutter forward and back

back and forward

on the old rocking chair

a heavy memory chair that used to support her grandmother

on the same porch only seven years ago, in the exact same spot

sure it had been awhile since grandma's much
publicized death

but faye just couldn't find it in herself to pitch
the chair

she wouldn't even let her husband lloyd sand
or paint it

even though he had moaned and groaned with
his big rumble voice

and waved his thick flabby arms to threaten
her frailty

saying that it was ugly and morbid to keep
around

how about a nice porch swing, for cryin' out
loud, huh

or at least let me fix it up and get those
bloodstains out

people in town are talkin'

let 'em flap their gums, I don't care

she would tell him flat faced and cold, the chair
stays

he would stomp around, go chop wood for the
woodpile

with his ridiculous huffs and grunts and red face

then come back through the screendoor of the
cabin

and stomp around some more

you're crazy, he'd say, craziest woman I ever met

I think it's time you get some help and i'm
serious

therapy or somethin' because you're just so, I
don't know

sick

and fucked up

really, faye, you're all sick and all fucked up

and not just cause of all your talkin' about
death

you rockin' in that chair is makin' me wanna
do bad things

rockin' chairs are for old people, you're thirty-
two

I didn't marry you so you can sit on your ass all
the time

one of these days, mark my words

i'm gonna toss that rickety old rocker in the fire

a real big fire and i'm gonna make you watch,
too

at this point in his tirade she usually tuned him
out

she'd heard it all before

she would just rock and smile and think of
grandma

just as she was rocking and smiling now

poor grandma, mauled to death by a black bear

in her dementia she had attempted to gather up
some cubs

the mother bear was furious

actually they said it was the bleedin' that killed
her

she managed to crawl away after the attack

all the way to the back porch

all the way into her rocker

that's where she bled out

in her favorite seat

she was clingin' stubborn to it when grandpa
came home

by then it was too late, the blood had dried, she
was gone

grandpa said that her awnry fightin' side did
her in

if she just woulda played dead then maybe

maybe she'd still be alive

or maybe not

she was very old

and poor grandpa, nature killed him, too

just a year after grandma died

he was walkin' along home from the graveyard

it was a terrible night in early april

a fierce ice storm had knocked out the power

and as the old man went slippin' along the
road in his work boots

a big long gone dead tree broke under the
weight of the ice

and whistled its way in a glistening crash onto
grandpa

knocked the hat off his head and the head off
his body

at first the local authorities couldn't even find
the head

it was way back in the woods

almost all eaten up

critters were rollin' it around in the crunchy snow

the northern woods were dangerous

and faye's lesson in nature danger didn't stop
there

the cabin was given to faye and her newlywed
lloyd

but her mother warned her to just sell if off

and use the money to get a place in the city

it's so much safer in the city, she'd say

but it was lloyd who bulldozed all decisions
the two made

faye could only protest meekly in her chin

down fashion

then two years later, a few days before

thanksgiving

faye's parents decided to drive up for the

weekend

well, daddy was at the wheel

daddy drove fast

a big deer leapt onto the road and froze in the

headlights

that was it

in the pulverizing snap of a finger

it was all over

they both died instantaneously

slamming into a ten-point buck

on the road to red jacket

faye wasn't the same after that

she became distant

spooky

she paid unhealthy attention to the woods

always there, right outside the window, heavy
and sinister green

always waiting, always hungry for more
fertilizer

the forest is full of death, she'd say

and lloyd would roll his eyes

goddamn you're nuts, the forest if full of life
and beauty

think hard about gettin' some help like I said

i'm sick of all this grim talk, we ain't movin', ever

at least get off that rocker and go for a walk, christ

take a long damn walk for all I care

squeak, squeak

ah, that sound

squeak, squeak

she snapped out of her recollections

finished her menthol cigarette

and rose from the blood dark rocker

with a devious wide-eyed smile

and a barely contained giggle

the bats

she twisted her hands together

the bats

were finally emerging

from her anxious lean on the paint chipped
wood rail

she could see them

popping their tiny twitchy heads out

from the crumbling boards of the garage

squeak and lunge and fluttering drop then fly

one by one they pushed out like monstrous babies

born into the night hungry, glittery eyed

their sonar goin' crazy

faye chewed on her bottom lip

digging her sharp white nails into the wood

excited!

bats carry all types of diseases, rabies and
maybe worse

she was rocking on her heels

nature danger

nature death

come on, bats, don't let me down, she called out

go get that cheese

there on the roof

go on, get it, free food

her excitement started to wane when she
realized

the bats weren't interested in the cheese

they weren't interested in the medium cheddar
meal

she had so carefully put out for them

and in such generous portions

they just looped off through the dark backyard
of trees

and away into the night

to the easy billowing feast of lamplight bugs
down in town

it surprised her a little that the bats didn't go
for the food

but then again, she didn't know too much
about bats

she just figured that they were ravenous mice
with wings

well damn, she slapped her hands on the rail

guess i'll just move right along with plan b

she went inside and took one of lloyd's beers
out of the fridge

one of his precious imported fancy pants
limited batch

obscuro raspberry cream nutmeg pale
whatever the fuck beers

she opened it, took a sip

it tasted awful

sure didn't taste like beer

she poured it out in a foaming swirl into the
grimy sink

old lloyd won't care, she said out loud

faye then went to the kitchen table

lloyd's cigarettes were there, half a pack

she lit one

at least his cigarettes tasted like cigarettes

stupid bats, they'd rather eat bugs then cheese, fine

she went back outside, onto the back porch,
across the backyard

over to the ladder, up the ladder, onto the
slanty garage roof

then she laughed

after all

lloyd did look pretty damn funny sittin' up there

gagged and hogtied and covered with cheese

he was naked except for the winding rope, his
boxer shorts

and the little bits of electrical tape she used to
secure the cheese

the only thing missing was a large silver platter

maybe a blood red apple in his mouth

a little pepper

a little salt

if seasoned correctly

somethin' would attack him sooner or later

she was sure of it

nature danger

nature death

but, oh well

the bats had left him alone

time for plan b

her husband's eyes were wild with wounded anger

his face red as he choked

on a stifled roar of insults under his rag mouth

hello lloyd

she blew a bit of smoke into his face

lloyd, in an amazing burst of strength, flipped
up once

like a desperate fish on wet carpet under an
empty fishbowl

he flipped as if to kick faye and then rolled like
a log

right off the roof and into the darkness below

faye, after descending the ladder to investigate

soon discovered that plan b was no longer
necessary

she went back to the rocker

looking out at the shadowy lump of lloyd in
the grass

a halo of flying bugs soon did gather

and faye waited patiently for nature to do its
thing

the softly spoken fish monologue

[*The imagined setting for this performance is in a modest theatre located in the northern woods, near or ideally above the 45th parallel. The theatre, although made of wood and holding the somewhat musty presence of a cabin, also retains the solemn air associated with some places of worship. Small altars containing taxidermy, pinecones and the like, are found along the walls, lit by flickering dedication candles. Slightly pungent and musky incense curls from canisters on the low stage. Alcohol and tobacco are permitted and encouraged. There is no dress code (although those who attend may feel compelled to wear their better outdoor attire). Windows are open, weather permitting, to the forest breezes*]

it will now be my pleasure

to take you

on a liquid travelogue

highlighting a few

of our multifarious and wondrous

fishes of the inland seas region

[speaker allows for applause, waits for them to cease]

yes, our multifarious

and wondrous

fishes of the inland seas region

they need us now

because by careless ballast

and by breeched canal

invasive species threaten

and by unholy waste dumping

and various pollutions

water quality diminishes

our favorite ectothermic vertebrates

may fail to find our frying pan one day

if we do not stand guard

wherever these cold waters flow

so let's go

there are many fish to see

some of them just might swim their way

deep into your dreams

twinkling enchanted splashings

happy dreams

but others may effect you like indigestion

they just may cause nightmares

blackish spiny fins and blood clouds

you never know

so the choice to continue

as always

is yours

[*a low muttering of grunted approvals ripple over
the crowd*]

i see

and so

we unmoor and our journey begins

in our deeper woods

of the farther north

where the slightest indications

of a rainy pond has gathered

see?

marshy and soft as the late afternoon clouds hover

cool with calm showers that splatter the
duckweed

imagine somber looming willows

reflected on the weedy surface

a weedy surface alive with the rippled hoops of
lightly falling rain

undulating the water lilies like the tickles of
invisible tiny hands

imagine we are there

in only a few inches

of tannin rich and tepid bog water

we can see movement in the shady soft bottom

not far from the mossy roots of a leaning
dogwood

yes, there she is, our very first fish

umbra limi

also known as the central mudminnow

a little lady with big brown eyes

she blends in quite nicely with the murk

the color of drenched and rotting tree bark

all splotched and mottled and quick to dash away

and how she twitches the daintiest of finspines

in constant preparation to flee from the various
beaked fiends

who ruffle feathers in the drizzle of dripping
branches above

*[speaker pauses, staring off in midair, squinting as a
new vision comes clear]*

and not far from our cautious little *umbra limi*

something else entirely stirs in the blurred and
turbid murk

belching slime bubbles from a silty blanket of
mud it rises

misshapen and rude in a cloud of shallow
disturbance

here comes our second fish

it is the rarely seen northern bogflutter

a warty blob with a big flapping frown of a mouth

he slurps rainy air at the surface

suspended there on a lazy palpitation of
primitive fins

filling the black balloon of his swim bladder

then down he sinks

    like some unfinished meal

to hide back in the muck as a brook stickleback
swims by

oh, the brook stickleback, such a silly little fish

it doesn't even see the lumpy bogflutter

but such obliviousness is to be expected

the brook stickleback, after all

has an oxygen deprived brain that it rarely uses

it can live in water where no other fish would survive

always seeking the shallows

the first fish on the spreading lip of a river flood

the stickleback is the type of creature

that nature has seemingly graced with baffling luck

because it has survived and thrived

in these drowsy waters for a very long time

and can always be easily identified by the
spiny rays

that grow from its back like inverted shark teeth

off it swims from the boggy pond

and to the edge of a weedy inland lake

where wood ducks twirl the surface

the idiot stickleback is seeking translucent bunches

of mosquito larvae to slurp

it flaps over the fallen and submerged tresses of
a willow branch

underneath which there hides three shy and
bony black crappies

[another pause, lake breeze through the conifer]

these particular crappies are all females of the
species

and these ladies wear perpetual frowns

they are darksome darlings who have little use
for the sun

but they are being drawn out of their hiding
place bit by bit

as the cloudy sky above darkens further with
the approaching dusk

you can see that both their fins and their scaly
flanks

are splattered with distinctive black spots

spots nearly as black as their brooding
thoughts

and with saucer eyes they reckon

a shadow form gliding by

the poetry of his sleepy motion is solemnly
regarded

it's a larger oily fish slow swerving towards the
creekmouth

           with tiny moustache dangling

it is none other than the selective benthic
omnivore known as carp

he makes his way along distracted by dreams
of distant asia

where his ancestors were rumored to have been
river kings

bringers of fortune and inspiration for samsara
fables

but now it has sadly come to this

it has come to

this obscured seven-foot ditch

deep in the northern woods

where there is nothing much to do

      but dive down

into an all too familiar feeding gallery

and suck up bottom mud

gloomy and sad

these lakes

and their waters

would humble any king in time

[speaker pauses once again, counting to five]

but not all whiskered creek dwellers are so blue

one big-mouthed lady fish in particular

seems to be less moody about her evolutionary

situation

she is a dark-skinned and yellow-bellied

gobbling catfish

known as bullhead

and she is visible not far from where the carp

is picking morsels from his mud clouds

she is waking up as the eventide in the world

above

ebbs closer and closer

she has a stout maternal shape and uses her

whiskers

as feelers to find her way

lady bullhead has lived in this creek through

five winters

and she bears strange scars

she has a bonified leading spine-like ray on her
dorsal and pectoral fins

and can lock these rays into place

so they prick outwards in defense

she can draw blood if not handled properly

those of you who cast a line

for these gluttonous gobblers know

but it is hard not to begrudgingly admire this
ugly daughter

as she rudely muscles her way face first
through the grassy shallows

grassy shallows that allow for all manner of
underwater personalities

there is, in fact

another creature here

another creature

you may not like at all

a true beastie who should be avoided at all
costs

indeed the most dreaded fish you will find

in a sluggish creek like this

strictly nocturnal and engorged vampiric by
sunrise

with blood purloined from sleepy cousins and
now headless turtles

it is none other than the malicious mahogany
fangtooth

waiting for darkness to fully descend

      before disembarking to dine

the fangtooth is a roundish monstrosity

mostly mouth

he can grow to the size of a small cabbage

sharp needle teeth and saucer eyes that can see
through the stygian

he feeds by clamping onto a victim and

inhaling the resulting red billows

and by the time the impaled victim is released

they are typically weakened and dazed

and more often than not they rise belly up to

the surface

perforated and drained

the mahogany fangtooth

is coming out of hiding a little early

with a flurry of vegetation

it lunges out for a smaller rainbow darter

[*speaker holds breath and places hand on heart*]

but the darter is too diurnal and quick for the

groggy bloodsucker

and off she flies with a twittering of her morsel-
sized heart

      off and away from the silty creek

      off and over the slightest of forest ridges

and into a braided tributary that threads to join
a warmer stream

which is the kind of flowing water the showy
little darter prefers

accelerated currents rolling a downgrade

through the woods where sandy riffles form

this is where the darter will feed on fish eggs

if they can be found

but see

the rain

above the riffles

as it intensifies

causing a breezy panic

at the surface

it has been raining for days now

and all the waterways swell

all water creatures, as you know,

are partial to soggy days like this

and in the deeper middle of the stream

there is a tasty pan fish

who seems to be in a particular stupor over the
downpour

he has cheeks streaked with aqua stripes

banded sides scattered with reddish dabs

and is commonly known

[brief pause, allowing audience to guess]

as a pumpkinseed

the striking pumpkinseed has very watchful
eyes

and he will linger after spawning

to use his watchful eyes

and defend his nest aggressively

he will even charge

and gallantly mouthfight

but spawning is over

his fry are gone

     our pumpkinseed yawns

         a rising silver thread of bubbles

stuporous indeed

and content

it is time to find some vegetation to float and

dream in

so he moves on his search

for a waving green sleep chamber

      for dreaming

      and dreaming

but the true royalty of this stream

the glorious brook trout

is not seeking some sleep chamber

she is seeking the swifter currents downstream

downstream past the leaping bluegill

where the water muscles apart

the banks along a sloping bend

to form a foaming rapids

with rushes and fast lappings over smooth grey
stones

a lovely foaming rapids

watched over by a stand of hundred year old
pine

this is where the lady trout

will practice the lashings of her legendary
caudal fin

the rapid splashing propel

and slap and shoot and fly she goes

that powerful rear fin and flapping tail that can
blast her forward faster

and faster than all of her natural predators

both in the water and hunting along the banks

like many lady fish she looks glorious when in
retreat and surely gone

she is too fast for you to fully admire

the creamy vermiculations on her slippery back

she is too fast and her instincts to survive are
too strong

she is a memorable fish

and the flashing vision of her getting away will
never leave you

and the brook trout motors ahead

and the brook trout flies and the brook trout is
gone

gone past the rapids where she lingered to play

gone into a slower moving expanse

that changes character

to become

a proper river

there are many fish

to be found here

[*another pause, the dull ringing of a bell from a sunken fishing boat*]

one of the most compelling river fish

in fact

is just ahead of us

racing along the banks and leaping every now and then

a bright flame licking up along the surface

slender and tapered

     small and fast

it is the riparian red

the fish famous

for driving hungry raccoon

and black bear furious

the riparian red is the most daredevil fish

in the whole watershed

he will swim directly at his much larger
predators

only to dart away from their gaping mouths

      leaving them nothing but twirling
ribbons of shit to snap at

this recklessness contributes to both the fish's
rather short lifespan

and to his ongoing popularity

among thrill seekers

sadly, however

you will rarely find a riparian red more than
three years old

let him go

just let him go

less glamorous

but no less important

is our next fish

we find him where the water deepens to seven feet

he is a slower fish and an easier meal

he is tiny

he is the mottled sculpin

poor little guy

his pectoral fins, face and mouth are all too big
for his body

and he wears a look of eternal earnestness and
gullibility

there is something about this particular fish, in fact

that makes almost all other fish of similar size
uncomfortable

these other fish seem to fear

that the sculpin's meekness might be
contagious

and they superstitiously give the spiny-rayed

fellow a considerable berth

but he is oblivious to all this

      and there he goes

swimming toward the mouth of the river

where the watery environment grows

suspiciously quiet

the sun has just dropped behind the tree line

night darkens the tranquil surface of the open bay

the atmosphere teeters between calm and

ominous

the rain has stopped

poor, poor little sculpin

he does not register the shadow rising hungrily

from beneath him

      he swims on confused and then

there is a rapid predatory lunge from his pursuer

and he is suctioned painfully

into a gaping mouth of needle-sharp teeth

there is no escape

he is swallowed whole to be digested slowly

his proteins and nutrients

converted to serve the further growth of his killer

the mighty and voracious

[*speaker traces large distinctive outline in the air*]

bowfin

an ancient species

the relatives of the bowfin hunted in prehistoric
waters

and dodged the thundering river crossings of
dinosaurs

her body is rangy and she is topped with a

dorsal fin of fifty rays

it resembles a long oily feather

and runs from her mid-back to her rounded tail

she is protected by scales that are nearly as
rigid as a washboard

and can survive weeks buried in the mud

this particular specimen is nine years old

moving towards a shoal

        because it is nightfall now

and in the waters by the shoal

near the alluvium of the river mouth

there are schools of bluntnose minnows

their shiny sides flash an iridescent silver

in the summery ghost glow of new moonlight

and they all look remarkably similar in their motions

just inches below the spooling

    velvet fluctuations

of the tingly waves

congregated together

    moving as one

they patrol the transitional shallows

between river and inland sea

and as we move through them

they scatter an open path for us

we bid farewell to the minnows as off we go

hugging the marshy bay shoreline

for one last look in the coastal coldwater

where we will meet two fish of similar

temperament and appetite

a tandem of toothy ambush predators from the
pike family

who have both made their home

in this paludial enclave

      near the arcing

slowly eroding horn

of a barrier peninsula

sloshing nickel steps beyond

silver rain furied cattails

the waters hold razors

ranged in the submerge

of fishy duckbills

day the rue

esocidae

the mean-assed pike family

ah, the stories…

voice popping over wind hissing

so wet your grey whistle

solemn your stone eyes

and listen

[*light on speaker fades, speaker grows indistinct*]

because we're past the pickerel

who are back there

under fallen branch dens

of smaller streams

so the larger pike are [*voice muffled by wind*]

more like cousins than brothers

angry boys both

you got your northern pike

smaller of the two

and you got your muskie

now the northern pike has wedged

his long projectile body in the weeds

while the wandering muskie

who, by the way, prefers deeper channels in
the open lake

but in truth can go wherever the hell he wants to

well, he has backed into the slippery hollows

of a submerged log

and there they both wait for their prey to pass

hovering motionless

glassy killer eyes twitching now and then

and then

when a smaller fish happens past

the lunging

and the gaping

and the snap

fish scales drifting off

like confetti in the murk

flashing silver and fading

both fish gone

vanished

in consumption and retreat

the mean-assed pike family indeed

sons of bitches will eat anything they can fit

[*muffling wind again*] mouths

this particular northern pike is just under two
feet long

while this particular muskie is about twice that size

the northern pike is greenish in color and the
more nervous of the two

the muskie is more muddy umber with dark
wavings

and a soft creamy belly

the northern pike have been known

to snap viciously at passing ghost fish

just as the muskie have been known

to strike at curious cats along the shoreline

fish mouth full of fur

but enough of these boys

there are deeper waters

for us to see

and so again

    here we go

    off into the expanse

of this coldwater lake

where the dreary waves are choppy

and where ocean bound barges sail

    solemn and grey

into what can be seen of the moonrise

frothy bones in their teeth

[speaker fades further in growing darkness]

way out there is a masculine fleet

of yellow perch in the deep eddies

they have strayed too far into the lake

and a panic possesses them

because even though they grow an inch a year
and can survive for ten

they are still just little men in a great big lake

of course in the glare of midday these fish are
very proud

they have well-developed jaws and they
flap them boldly

you should hear some of the condescending
boasts they bray

but when darkness falls their schools
quickly unravel in fear

the yellow tinges on their fins
lose their luster

and they stop their jaw
flapping to run and hide

but they are not fast enough for
the walleye

oh, the walleye

he is a vicious and voracious carnivore

and he snatches a yellow perch from the
dissolving fleet

he snatches that yellow perch head-first and
screaming

the perch tail flaps wildly in his mouth

but soon falls still with a toothy crunch

this walleye is only satisfied

     in the fleeting moments when he is
feeding

he weighs thirteen very unlucky pounds

thrives in darker waters

his creepy eyes reflect light demonically

and as soon as he swallows one perch

that formidable masticator is off

      looking for another

   deeper

fifty feet down

   deeper

one hundred feet down

deeper still

two hundred feet down

where the water is frigid

here you can find

the lake whitefish

elegantly floating

in the slow ether loops

of a solitary blue ballet

silver-sided and sleek

simple in design

she has a subterminal mouth

with a rounded humble snout

this bashful whitefish

can claim these waters

like few others

her sisters have navigated

these quiet depths

since they were born

in ice by glacial carving

many centuries ago

the thunder of louder fish

never shakes her

so she descends

another fifty feet

deeper

two hundred and fifty feet down

deeper

three hundred feet down

deeper still

three hundred and fifty feet

below the surface

the weight of the water above

heavier and pressing

here we find

the downward sloping lake floor

where a strange primeval lady

is prowling the sand

[*speaker disappears completely*]

her back is ridged like armor

with rows of hard plates

she is a sifting

slow moving bottom-feeder

six feet long

a member of the reclusive set

known as lake sturgeons

how long has she been swimming

all the way down here?

as long as ninety-seven summers

counted by calendar year

see the ages reflected

in her cloudy eyes

no other fish in her lake

or in any of its root spread of tributaries

has eyes as unnerving as this two-hundred pound elder

she has an extended snout

that flattens into a shovel shape

and a pair of sensory barbels drooping

she gulps her various food bits whole

because she has no teeth

she has never had any teeth

the great queen lake sturgeon

follows a dramatic sloping plunge

   descending into the blackened depths

four hundred feet down

  deeper

five hundred feet down

   deeper

     over six

      well over

    six

      hundred

       feet

     down

    there

   on a slight ridge

  lies a shipwreck

   wreck

    wreck

no fish but the lake sturgeon

no fish but the lake sturgeon

to see

it is a nineteenth

century

sinking

broken apart

in a gale

and here

she lies

her bulkhead

blasted

     a single strand

of her tattered sail

   still waving

      waving

        waving

     but the icy

       silver and shiver

        and shiver

    the rolling

      depths

   the frigid wavings

     have preserved

 the solid bones

of her sailors

and uneaten

hard tack

tack

tack

can still

be found

if you

sift through

the surrounding

sands

carefully

but if you ever do

investigate this place

for treasure or grim trinkets

do so knowing

that this is a place

of considerable danger

because there is one final fish

to consider

    before we extinguish

      for the night

    one final fantastic creature

a wellspring of legend

    a watery widow maker

      snaring ships

on stormy nights

    consuming crew

      and cargo alike

    she is real

and she is down there

[final pause, counting to nine, sound of the water]

all seven hundred pounds of her

she is there buried

in the silt below

the cracked board wreckage

of that old ship

and she is the strangest

most colossal organism

in this or any lake

close your eyes

and look

there

through the gaping monster hole

in the damaged ghost heavy hull

through the slow-motion seaweed beds

waving and waving so slow

and in the dreams

of sleepy sailors

still alive

and slumbering

and in the shoreline campfire smoke

that rises for the telling of tales

and in the water somewhere

and in the water

hold your breath

close your eyes

and look

there

we see a roping coil of something

it looks like some large eel

but it is neither eel nor hagfish

it is merely the feeling tip

of this creature's suction cup tentacle

she has nine of these

emerging in sets of three

from either side of her horrible

red funnel mouth

a sucking hole centered

in a pulsating bed of razor teeth

waiting as red as a floating rose

or sunken valentine

waiting for any food

to drop

down

she is a rare hunter

but when hunger demands

she will rise

rest assured

she will rise

she will extend her tentacles

ever so slowly

one at a time

bracing herself on the sunken ship

and nearby boulders

and she will lift herself free from the sand

in a towering cloud

the cloud obscures her

but you can see the red eyes glowing

and you can see tentacles flapping

as she takes off

through the darkness

and down

down deeper

than moonlight

can reach

seven hundred

feet down

silvery bubbles

trailing after her

deeper she goes

eight hundred

feet

down

deeper still

nine hundred

feet

down

and deep

deep

into leagues

and fathoms

of sleepy sleepy

sleep

passion by darkness

last night

margie was planning to have

a nice, quiet evening to herself

she made a small dinner

turned the television face to the wall

and lit some cinnamon red candles

rolled out that winter blanket

trying hard to decide

well what should I do

finish that book

or write those letters

or make that call home

she heaved a frustrated sigh

she was distracted

couldn't seem to focus on any of those things

her wide fleshy hips

kept moving, twitching

a warm tingle began to bother her

she rose from her cozy chair

and went to the top drawer of her dresser

there was only one thing in that drawer

rested on a heart shaped be my valentine satin
pillow

was danny boy, her vibrator

she smiled, picked it up

then

she frowned

shit, no

this won't do

not tonight

she put danny boy back on his pillow

for future battery powered engagements

and picked up her silver phone

dialed seven numbers to one man

her boy luke picked up

and with her most sultry

come hither purr

she said

come over

precious boy

I am in need

this is a very

very urgent and special

need

that I have

make haste, precious boy

don't make me wait

and don't you dare tell me

that you have other plans

nothing could be as important

as this

she was touching herself

luke gripped the phone

he began to sweat

he liked big, round women

and margie was very big and very round

of course I will

he said

will you wear

that dimestore tiara in your hair

and that egyptian eye make-up, honey child

yes she said

I am your cleopatra

and I promise

to let no asp near my bosom

I will save my breasts for you

but you must shave for your queen

and be sharp and clean for your queen

and most important of all

be hungry when you show up

and be here within the hour

yes he said

i'll see you soon she said

and then

once again

cold rolling

leisurely revolving

the stage

both shadow-curtained

and inflammatory

was set

the cities, one by one

donned their flickering capes

darkness chased over the globe

and with that quiet

low hum

some call silence

you could hear

flesh alive

generating new heat

in the absence of the sun

luke was rushing to get ready

he had margie's picture taped

up on his bathroom wall

her toss of chestnut hair and frozen laugh

caught in summertime

her bed appeared in his mind

warm sheets peeling back by themselves

a breeze blowing dead petals across the

whiteness

he shaved quickly in his undershirt

blue veins rising in the flex of his biceps

suspenders hanging and an erection in his

trousers

checking his reflection in a cloudy mirror

dipping his razor in a soapy glass of water

thinking of margie and her smile

and

her tongue

his heart was thumping with a starlit darkwash

behind him the setting sun tossed another date

away like a dried-up leaf

drift and glide and float

to the tremble of the floor

and there it smoldered

forming in its flutter of overcast ashes

the promise of a tremor and a tryst

a plush molten heartbeat stew

a thrust and swell of blood

a divine slippery feast

margie tilted her head back to apply eyeliner

her cigarette sending smoke signals from the
ashtray

she already had her hair piled high

and that dimestore tiara perched trashy there

she was thinking of her luke

thinking that a biblical name suits him

thinking that a certain

excitable extension of his manly anatomy

was indeed very biblical in its proportions

very very biblical, she licked her lips

outside her apartment window the serpentine
highways

went slipstream and rumble under the winter
blue

all things obliquely sliding towards decay,
demise

margie pulled up her black stockings on the
edge of her bed

very much alive

dreaming of shivery feathertip touches

of uncorked laughter above

and creaking bedsprings

of a deep rhythm

very much like love

an ongoing skin and bone symphony

swirling the windy grey bearded clouds

dancing the stars

lifting the rocky moon

in the frozen immensity of the heavens

revealed by blue light and black space

luke drove his car quickly to margie's
apartment

the winter city and it's tall buildings

went twinkle twinkle

beneath that rippling reversed pool of the night
sky

that glides on in wondrous motion

issuing highblown whispers

like silver white with their eyes then fingers
then mouths

the lovers began to converge and strike and roll
in city smoke tinderboxes with a gush of flame
and burn and luke mounted the stairs to
margie's apartment in leaps and bounds in his
flapping overcoat and tie to ring her buzzer
where she emerged in her short tight green skirt
and red heels and green mascara and red lips
and he said merry christmas and she grabbed
him by his tie and pulled him inside where they
met in a hungry sensual kiss, she lifted her big
thigh leg and pressed into him, delicious and his
eyes closed, the dimly lit radiator hot room was
quickly sucked away into oblivion by quick
pulse amnesia as she grinded him back into the
wall, something fell and broke, a picture frame
perhaps, no matter, their feverish heads turned
to poppy dustbowls dry and sparked and
blazing with sweltering flashes as lifeblood

gravity dropped to labia flowers in their engorged wet velvety blooms between thighs of brackish sweat and the stiff hoist of male arousal met them hip to hip and his fingers tickled their way up the inside of her black stocking thighs to find her wet right through and he fell to his knees and licked the fabric there, saying la la my naughty mistress of the nile you taste, ooh la la so sweet and she bit her lip and grabbed a handful of his hair as he battled her stockings, pulling them down with a hard ripping grunt and yank and down the street a building had burst into flames and firetrucks and emergency vehicles raced to the scene and that old devil moon had slipped down from its cold roost and was pounding on the roof with a big maniacal green cheese grin and luke was licking those full pouty lips with a chin dripping nectar, my love, luke said and yes she said, and then she fell forward pushing him down to the floor where she covered his mouth with kisses while her hands freed his belt and freed his zipper and

freed his manhood, something miraculous
happened to the candle flames, they elongated
and grew higher as if a voyeuristic spirit had
entered the room to watch this sloppy tango and
the sirens wailed and people were shouting and
the lovers met hip to hip and skin to skin and lip
to lip, buttons sent flying like castaway nickels
or skipping stones, straps and neckties and
scarves and belts and socks and shoes all
loosened and lost, breathing rose from the
smoke and electric cold of shadow places with
the universal sighs of pant and moan and
prayer, the stone echo of city bridges, the grind
and push and tender touch and grind and push
again in dark hallways and master bedrooms
and leaking ratholes and the corks and bubbly
and aching cocks and muscle strain and sweat
and lift and groove and wet slides and slaps and
the sirens get louder, the flames get higher and
luke has wrestled margie onto the couch where
the bent arrow of the servant has found the
welcoming bullseye of the queen, that stiff pillar

swaying into the thick sappy hot gush and she is saying please, oh, oh danny boy, I mean luke, yes, oh luke, you biblical bastard you, sing passion by darkness and he is moaning oh you delicious little strumpet and the lanterns on the ship all were swinging and the wind was thunder and she was grabbing his ass with the up and down and the oil of almonds and the brain soft like opium and the honey dust and the ineffable bliss and the clocks started to melt and sizzle on the quaking walls and then they rolled off the couch with a smear of cushions and a lamp fell and she rolled him over and said oh babylon, oh city of veils and his strong hands slammed her hips down and in and out and in and the silverware rattles and the floors whine and sway and then

yes, oh yes

they come

loudly

with oh god moans

that biblical flood of fire had rippled to
overflow

the foamy jet and the claws raking skin

the wails and the sighs

the damp, clinging bodies

the arson anointed skin

bodies still locked

heaving

the embrace

and the melt

a milky flood of semen

a retreating tremble

of vaginal muscles

quick breaths

returning to normal

and the languor

the soft

soft kisses

the smiles and laughter

a cigarette

a dizzy walk to the bathroom

and margie came back in her robe

tiara still amazingly halfway on

luke smiled

opened the wine

let's drink to that

he said

and hell yeah

she said

the misty brook

long ago

during a much more

enchanted stretch of time

there lived all manner of creature

in the woodsy stretch of woods

down by the misty brook

and all summer long the lanterns would be lit
at day's end

to sway an attraction for fireflies and such

and you could always find

almost without fail

some friends

a frolic

and a frothy drink

ah, the summer woods

so beautiful

but I should point out

that much of the green beauty that
summertime knows

owes a great deal to how quickly it draws to a
close

and when the first mischievous cold little
zephyr

flies in from the north hissing rumors of icicles
on the way

and when the trees all shiver to acknowledge
this new chill

and the nacreous crackling frost

conspires and gathers by moonlit sparkles

to leave its glistening bewares

in a colder and somehow more golden sunrise

all reasonable voices acknowledge

that autumn has arrived

that enchanted time when fat pumpkins

ripen to plump all orange from their terrestrial
vines

the time of fallen acorns, shiny buckeyes and
fresh cider

the time to chop the knotty wood, bake warm
treats and knit scarves

and creatures called by instinct to either
migrate or hibernate

all reckon the need to burrow and bolster and
muster and post haste

down in the woodsy stretch of woods

down by the misty brook

the passing of summer will always inspire

the slimy, furry and feathered

to hop, scurry and fly in the frenzy of their
winter preparations

nodding to each other as they pass on the
sylvan path

huffing to haul overflowing pushcarts of red
apples back home

they whistle and work away because there is
no time to waste

such a bustle beneath the maple red and the
sycamore moon

and like witches on oily brooms

the days fly to the far side of halloween

and it was on one of these breezy days

in the breezy month of november

that the bright but chilly morning sun

was shining through the little window

carved and bayed and circular

down in the mossy tree stump

that flippy the frog called home

he was wearing his red sweater and he was
whistling a tune

his sunrise tea was steeping

as he busied himself around his bed with
pillow fluffing and such

because, after all, comfort and warmth are a
bed's two great necessities

especially when a frog has to spend five
months asleep there

that is a very comfortable and warm bed, he
declared

and after one final day of work I will sleep my
way through the snow

so he finished his bedtime preparations and
sipped his teacup empty

then stretched his little arms

did several huffing leg bends

put on his little red cap

holstered his six shooter

and went out into the day with a smile

down the woodsy trail he traveled

on a breezy promenade along the misty brook

when all of a sudden, just past a prickly thicket

he spied the dapper and dour sebastian the
cricket

standing with impeccable posture by the
flaking log that he called home

sebastian had stepped outside to light his pipe

and regard the blustery day

he hailed his familiar frog acquaintance with a
regal nod

then removed his tiny watch and chain from
his tiny vest pocket

and, apparently satisfied with the hour of their
meeting,

nodded regal once again

my dear sir flippy, he said then cleared his
throat, a good day to you

flippy squared his shoulders and pointed his
green finger

you shut up, he said

i've had to endure your repetitive leg saws all
summer long

how many nights i've been forced to lie there
sleeping while you whine

and in your mind you imagine that you are an
entire symphony but no

you, my dear cricket, have always been more
pretentious than talented

oh, such harsh words from flippy!

the sudden dropping of sebastian's jaw

caused his pipe to fall to the ground

and there it smoldered lightly in the dry leaves
until he stomped it out

if you do not take more care with your tongue,
young frog, he bristled

then I may seek satisfaction by challenging you

to a duel in black crow meadow

flippy responded to the threat with a snarl

and then sprang with a great leap

to knock the cricket backwards with tumble
down force

flippy then hoisted hard on the long musical
legs of sebastian

until they popped off

and from his newly emptied hip pivots

there now oozed a nauseating yellow muck

the cricket screamed terribly as crickets who
lose their legs will do

until he was silenced by a concussive battering
from the murderous frog

who beat poor sebastian to death with his own
still twitching limbs

you could hear the wails go sailing above

the woodsy stretch of woods

down by the misty brook

flippy then removed sebastian's head with a
clean twist and pull

to have something to kick along the trail

while he meditated on his murder

that felt quite good, he said to himself

I wonder what fool will be next to cross my
path

as he rounded a corner he wound up and
kicked the head one final time

and it bounced and rolled all soggy until it
came to a stop

right in front of peter possum who sniffed
curiously at it then shrieked

I recognize this as the noggin of sebastian the
cricket, he said

and this implies my cricket friend is
irretrievably dead

my god, what a terribly awful and awfully
terrible thing to happen!

thus he did lament awhile and fret while a
furtive wind did blow

and flippy took advantage of peter possum's
distracted dismay

by picking up a nearby rock and sneaking up
behind him

oh so deviously

oh so quietly

all furtive and stealth and then

with the deepest deep breath

he possibly could heave

and with all the strength

his skinny frog arms could muster

he brought the rock down to pound

crack and slam on peter possum's cranium

and then as you may guess or know

poor peter crumbled beneath the vicious blow

then flippy lifted with a snarl to crack and slam
again

whistling all the while he cheerfully
bludgeoned away

until these mad smashings

at long last

left him

hovering breathless

sapped of strength and a wee bit bloody to boot

over a possum skull dashed to nothing more
than gore covered fragments

flippy huffed the killing rock off into the dry
grass

then paused awhile to gather up the kindling of
his broken thoughts

brittle and flammable and begging to be set
ablaze

in that woodsy stretch of woods

down by the misty brook

such a homicidal racket

was a shock to the autumn stillness

and venerable lord ashton the squirrel

from his piney roost in a nearby spruce

was the first to react to the commotion

he gathered up his ornate and polished rapier

then onward he came rushing with a monocle
pressed to his eye

worried that there might be a need to send up a
warning

to signal a new danger that had darkened the
morning

perhaps the wolf has returned and the whole
vicinity must be alerted

perhaps the old clapper in that rusty wolf bell
must be struck once more

worry and trepidation sought to hinder his
way

but venerable old lord ashton found courage in
the faith

that his prowess with a foil in fencing would
defend him

so with his saber in hand he went rushing
down the trail

bushy tail jerking in spasms of excitement

but when he came to the scene of the crime

he found no wolf

on the contrary and much to his surprise

the sight of flippy the frog greeted his eyes

and his great bushy tail ceased its jerking

flippy smiled at lord ashton and smiled at lord
ashton's saber

then he brought out his long barreled six
shooter

and fired a shot that caused the foolish squirrel
to tumble and wail

flippy then hopped over and pistol whipped
him until he wailed no more

blood speckling his face

his laughing smile

well, he decided, that was easier than pouring
cider in a cup

and since I have five bullets left I should use
them all up

he stroked his chin pensively and considered
possible victims

there were so many annoying animals he
would rather not see

when he awoke again in the dripping thaw of
the muddy spring

there is much to do, he said, and much to get
done

so with new resolve a gleeful flippy hopped on
down

to the water's edge where he rinsed his red
hands clean

the gore leaving his amphibious skin in
coldwater clouds

that drifted under spinning dead leaves
downstream

carried off by the shallow flow

of the tranquil misty brook

then he wiped his hands dry

did a few more leg bends

and looked up

big white clouds rolled by overhead

and the sky was a very deep and enviable blue

it was then that he heard the voice of rosie the
robin above him

hello flippy and flippy goodbye

because off I must go and off I must fly

but I will return on the airy lift of april breezes

as i'm known to do

and on my return I will be looking forward to
seeing fine folk like

pop went flippy's pistol before rosie could
finish her rhyme

and the red feathers on her breast darkened
further

with the leaking freshness of a heart pumped
stain

and gasping she fell splat from her willow tree
perch

yanked by gravity to rudely crash

where phallic mushrooms sprouted from the
frosty earth

flippy hopped over and saw that she had
landed beakdown

and that her twitchy feet were still twitching

so he aimed his pistol slowly with an eye
squint

and planted a bullet right where her wings met,
bang

tendrils of smoke rose from the fatal wound

and rosie the robin moved no more

flippy took a series

of deep, deep inhales

and exhales

and inhales

and exhales

and in a few brief minutes

a dream had come true

he had eliminated four

of the most annoying creatures he knew

in the woodsy stretch of woods

down by the misty brook

and what was more

he felt remarkably little remorse

until cuddles the porcupine came trundling
foolishly along

to see the bodies of peter possum, lord ashton
and rosie all dead

and also what appeared to be a severed
cricket's head

he cried oh flippy, oh flippy, what have you
done?

and flippy reluctantly replied with the end of
his gun

the loud echo of the cracking shot bounced
from tree to tree

and after the numb auditory shock of the blast
faded

and the wispy smoke vanished into an invisible
acrid scent

flippy noticed that his shot had only grazed the
side of cuddle's head

with spiny backside all quivering in a
lumbering and wounded retreat

the dim-witted porcupine was scurrying off

and spurting a red trail behind him

flee, instinct commanded, flee and fast and
save your hide

so cuddles ran and ran and continued running

with six words pouring from his lips over and
over

flippy is on a homicidal rampage

flippy is on a homicidal rampage

the gusty wind, as if trying to aid his escape

lifted a blazing curtain of leaves behind him

and for a few rather nervous moments flippy
lost sight of his prickly prey

and then, ah yes, he came back into view

after bumping into the trunk of a walnut

there he stopped running

and instead just swayed in a state of babbling
trauma

feeling the side of his head then looking
bewildered at his dripping paws

until finally

some new sense of his situation caused him to
scream repeatedly

flippy caught up to him and this time made no
mistake

firing off his last two shots eye to eye at point
blank range

cuddles the porcupine fell dead

hitting the ground in a crackling shudder of
quills

flippy finally felt an ephemeral pang

of bona fide remorse

poor cuddles is just too much of a dunce to
keep a secret, he said

and all witnesses who cannot be trusted must
be eliminated

because survival always nullifies friendship for
the solitary killer

it is the meditative chant of omerta

all animals are enemies and all animals must be
dead

and there is quite simply nothing more to be
said

and thence a challenging day turned even more
challenging

in the woodsy stretch of woods

down by the misty brook

now the element of surprise would be gone

now the rest of the animals would come
surveying and alert

and upon seeing the mayhem

and with justifiable caution

they would rush off to protect themselves

and in every surreptitious flittering amongst
the fallen leaves

they would detect something loathsome and
bloodthirsty

all would now be on their guard

flippy knew that he would have to return

to his home-stump for awhile

to let the woodland simmer

until his moratorium on hunting was through

he lofted his empty pistol into the briar along
the way

then with froggy hands clasped together he
paused to pray

oh please may the elemental forces that govern
the nature of life

abide with me through the rest of my perilous
and bloody day

and imbue me with the unbridled vigor that is
so very necessary

to battle past what is verboten

and then vanquish

all those who have vexed me for oh so long

when he stopped his prayer he heard a panic of
voices

he listened intently

he heard voices he knew

murder most foul, one was crying out, murder
by the misty brook!

flippy then rushed back home and climbed in
bed

he pulled on his tasseled sleeping cap and got
under his woolen blankets

then closed his eyes and brought back the
images of the day

how singular and sanguine are the recollections
of one who decides to kill

to have the terrified eyes of an array of victims
burned into the brain

eyes that wheel in a frantic slideshow

all losing their glow as death arrives

it is an intoxicant that brings a bitter taste

and deep trouble to most soldiers

but that killers swill happily

like pickled connoisseurs and rollicking drunks

flippy kicked his frog legs restlessly under the
covers

the mental frenzy that lingered from his
murders

made it impossible to relax

he had to finish what he started

there would be no naptime today

so he filled a satchel with lethal implements

then headed back out

whistling and high-stepping as if nothing had
happened

unfortunately he had forgotten to wash off the
gore of his rampage

and thus his whistling and high-stepping
looked rather demented indeed

as he made his way through

the woodsy stretch of woods

down by the misty brook

when his skipping carried him to the water's
edge

he saw the mossy back of shelly the turtle

with her head, arms and legs pulled in she was
apparently hiding

flippy stopped his whistling and hopped up on
her shell

who's there, she asked nervously,

is it the frothing beast who has been on the
loose?

flippy laughed, now, shelly,

would a frothing beast identify himself as
such?

flippy, she said, is that the voice of flippy the
frog I hear?

he hummed and dug around in his satchel

it most certainly is, dear terrapin

oh, you silly frog, came the muffled voice of the
turtle

you should be hiding like me

flippy lifted a hatchet from his satchel

and held it up in the sunlight, what?

I said you should be hiding somewhere like me

what?

I said there is a killer on the loose and you
should be hiding

shelly, won't you pop your head out

and speak so that I can hear you properly?

the turtle apologized, said of course

her compliance to his request

as you may have guessed

left her rudely decapitated

a great gush of bright red spluttered out from
the neck stump

then a final death spasm made the entire shell
convulse and shudder

the bright red faucet flow consequently
diminished to a bubbling trickle

which flippy realized sounded very much

like the bubbling trickle of the misty brook
itself

he groped around in his satchel and found a
sturdy rope

then hopped newly sinister and lopsided under
the weight of his deeds

down a braided trail that hissed with the
restless dry shifting of cattails

to where he knew he would find sweet ruby
raccoon

ah yes, sweet and adorable ruby raccoon

she lived in the prettiest little yellow treehouse
you might imagine

and it was nestled in the supporting crooks and
slingshot beams

that can always be found

in the sprawling branches of old pin oaks

flippy ascended the handy slat ladder ruby had
nailed to the trunk

and there he summoned a hyperventilating
panic

with a ruse of false jitters and panting he
urgently rapped

knock, knock, knock with the leafy iron garland
knocker

that was mounted for summons on the old
lady's door

miss ruby, he cried, miss ruby, he shouted

that i'm being pursued by a madman cannot be
doubted

he's been in pursuit of me and on my heels

all through this woodsy stretch of woods

down by the misty brook

please, oh, please, let me in or suffer to hear my
dying screams

and thus he did knock

and thus he did holler

and he did so for quite some time

but if ruby was inside

she made not a peep

well, fuck it, flippy said

and he ceased his unsuccessful and clamorous
deception

to thoughtfully smear some blood that was
drying on his chin

it was now his task to contrive some new

and perhaps more direct approach

after a few brief moments of thought he lifted a
finger to express

that he'd acquired some new inspiration to
solve his unexpected setback

and then he climbed right back down the tree
and dug in his duffle again

this time he pulled out a saw and hopped right
to work

see-sawing back and forth viciously on the
trunk

while november breezes coasted

all various and sibilant through the shaking
branches above

the sawdust and tiny chips of his toils sprayed
out

as he lustily belabored the frightened oak with
his cutting

until at long last it creaked and was sent
sideways timber cracking

snapping branches and twigs along the way

and thus with great arboreal chaos it crashed to
the woodsy floor

with a great billowing whoosh of red leaves

and in the tangle of this senseless lumbering

you could see what was left of ruby's pretty
little yellow house

all smashed and splintered accordion style

as if stepped on by the boot of some malicious
giant

flippy tossed aside his saw

rubbed his hands together in a villainous way

and once again picked up his sturdy rope

then loping through the new wreckage he
sought out his victim

calling ruby, oh ruby, where can you be?

and when he found her pinned and still
moving

beneath a very uncomfortable and prickly
thatch of broken branches

he noosed the rope around her neck then lifted
to strangle

causing her tongue to pop out in a decidedly
nauseating fashion

in her choking she made a flurry with her little
black hands

and that was the last little flurry she ever made

before she joined the growing ranks of the dead

in the woodsy stretch of woods

down by the misty brook

after flippy finished off that old raccoon

he paused awhile to stretch and yawn

his unavoidable hibernation, you see

was coming on

time is short now

soon I must rest

time is short now

but my winter nap

is still a few hours away

there's more blood to spill

before the end of the day

it made him wonder how much death

might be like his motionless overwintering

did those he killed just drift through deeper

channels of sleep now

deep and rich with a constant flow

of untethered and never-ending visions?

ah, death the great mystery

death the big question mark

and death the almighty release

flippy made a greenish furrow of his brow

and all of this thinking about death

naturally led him to think of mabel the owl

a bird of prey he'd wanted to prey upon for

quite some time

so he made his way with nefarious satchel in

tow

and along the way he reckoned

that he was the most satanic in the order

salientia

and that any other goddamn frog

from any other goddamn pond or stream

would most certainly shorten their life by

crossing paths with him

after all

only a raving fool

would fail to respectfully acknowledge

that he was the most fearsome and ferocious

and draconian creature by far

in the woodsy stretch of woods

down by the misty brook

so when he found the sycamore where mabel
the owl lived

he wasted no time in heaping piles of dead
leaves outside her door

then he produced the orange flicker that signals
the birth of a flame

through the providential rubbing

of nearby sticks

and after a wisp of white

a little orange smolder

and a little yellow sizzle

whoosh, the dead leaves went up in a flash

soon the fire grew fierce and bright

flippy squinted in the crackling glare and could
clearly hear

the sounds of an owl besieged by terror coming
from inside

he heard pieces of furniture being knocked
over

the rattle of pans and the nervous flapping of
wings

which of course just billows and tends to
worsen such things

moments later mabel the owl opened her
sizzling latch

with a little scream

and hurled her burly frame through the inferno
but only to her peril

because soon her feathers all flared up

and the way she smelled reminded flippy why
owl

is not a popular dish in most restaurants

he tracked her scorched path down to the
water's edge

where he saw the old bird collapse

and expire in a blackening heap on the shore

when the screaming finally stopped

it was peaceful

he found one of his favorite rocks to sit upon

and there he sat right down and yawned

and stretched

the tension melting from him

in the waves of heat

the flames gently crackling

with a campfire calm

he thought of white marshmallows twisted on
damp twigs

he thought of his first days as a young frog

just after the last remnants of his tadpole tail
had fully retreated

he thought not only of nocturnal campfires and
ghost stories told there

but of a sunny childhood spent on lazy-time
lily pads

dreamily watching white lotus blossoms

there was an innocence

yes, there was a beauty to those days

a romanticized simplicity flippy now strained
to recall

with a sigh of loss and frustration

he figured those days were gone for good

some killers have childhoods of misfortune

which not only drive them to mayhem

but which prepares them

for the spiritual trauma of their bloody
conquests

flippy, strange as it may seem, had no such
history

he had grown up very happy

it wasn't until he spent years living with his
neighbors

that his cheerfulness darkened and in the
nursery of this new darkness

there grew a sadness and then out of this
sadness

there grew an anger

directed at those who had compromised his
happiness

and out of that anger

directed at those who had compromised his
happiness

there grew a resentment and then out of that
resentment

there grew a loathing that eventually turned
corrosive and foul

still, in spite of the certainty he was most
definitely damned

he couldn't help but recognize

that it was truly an exquisite november day

the sun had few clouds to compete with

and even though the blown smoke of mabel's
burning

dimmed the sunny sparkles on the water

there was still much natural beauty to be
admired

in that woodsy stretch of woods

down by the misty brook

but his meditation was interrupted

by the bubbling of bubbles on the surface of the
water

he knew very precisely and without a doubt

it was that colossal asshole

thaddeus the trout

so with a new and infernal invigoration

flippy rummaged his satchel again and found

something small yet heavy and black and
round

he hefted it playfully from one webbed hand to
the other

ah, such a wonderful device

and if you can't guess what this device was

well

i will tell you

it was a tightly packed and lethal gunpowder
bomb

beautiful in its simplicity because simple was
its purpose

the creator having both conceived and
constructed it

to do nothing more than blow a wide variety of
things to bits

and flippy had been made aware by books on
the topic

that it would work exceedingly well on all
kinds of fish

so when the bubbles that announced the arrival
of thaddeus the trout

intensified and gathered as that big talker rose
clueless to the surface

the frog lit the pig tail curl of the short wick

and it hissed with a steady burning

it caused him to rear back and grimace and
squint

now you may be wondering why flippy was so
confident

that thaddeus would promptly rise to greet his
own destruction

so at this point it will serve you well

to remember that it pays to be observant

and a certain frog had been forced to observe

the behavior of this trout all summer long

every time he tried to take a nap by the
peaceful gurgle of those waters

that goddamn trout would rise up

and pop his head out and blab and blab

well, this time flippy had something that
would fit nicely

in that tiresome pie hole

moments later thaddeus appeared as predicted

with his head all shiny and wet

saying what are you doing dear frog and how
have you been

and oh, the weather and oh, the coming freeze
and oh, is that a bomb?

yes, said flippy

and with a wheeling big league wind up

he delivered a whizzing sparkler pitch

and with a slushy thud it landed right in the
gaping trap of that trout

seconds later the head of thaddeus blew apart
with an earsplitting boom

and his headless fish body sank gracefully
down

trailing clouds of guts which were gobbled up

with an unnerving quickness by his finned
brothers

down went the trout to the cool rocky bottom

of the misty brook

the satchel was now empty

and flippy decided that he would make one
more attempt

to take a little nap before his final kill of the
season

one final brief siesta before his long hibernation

just a short little late autumn and late afternoon
slumber

he certainly felt that he had earned it

because homicide, after all, can be an
exhausting business

and the woodland creature he'd left for last

bucky the beaver

was not the type to go down easy

but, oh, thought flippy, he most certainly will
go down

that saw-toothed busy body whose obsession
with damming

caused him to work noisily into the night

more than any of the others

that motherfucker had to go

so off he hopped for home and set his alarm for
sundown

that was the proper time for such business

the sable rolls of eventide

the long shadows which allow further stealth
to wicked deeds

the big clouds over the moon and a concealing
night mist

that's what he would wait for

yes, that's when bucky the beaver would die

now bucky was a burly and hairy chap

and his gruff manner and industrious drive
kept him from socializing

furthermore he harbored a contempt for
creatures who wasted time

time that could otherwise be spent in the
productive assembly of things

he had no patience for those who loitered

nor did he suffer the company of dawdlers or
gossipers

and thus while his work was almost always on
schedule

he was also, more often than not, painfully
misinformed

especially concerning events that did not
immediately involve him

and even though he had certainly heard

some unexpected outbursts through the day

horrible screams and trees falling and bombs
exploding and such

he never thought to seek out the source of these
rackets

there was too much work to get done

especially with the snow so soon to fall

in the woodsy stretch of woods

down by the misty brook

so bucky the beaver worked through the
afternoon

and bucky the beaver worked until the sun
went down

and then bucky the beaver worked some more
by lantern light

gathering twigs and branches and chomping
logs into usable shapes

it was exhausting to watch

and where he managed to get so much energy
was anyone's guess

it was hard to tell if old bucky ever bothered to
stop and rest

as he labored and muttered to himself in the
rigors of his toil

until in the spooky hour that precedes the
ominous tolling of midnight

he heard a rustling in the breezy dark scatter of
leave piles

he slowed down to listen

what could it be?

a frosty november moon commanded the
lugubrious night clouds to part

and that troublesome rustling repeated itself

twigs snapping to signify a creeping approach

in the nervous shadows that lined the chilly
brook

bucky listened and listened

then with great annoyance he ceased arranging
the branches of his dam

picked up his lantern and decided to have
himself a look

it was then that flippy sprang into view

wearing a black cape

and brandishing a wicked curved butcher knife

which he plunged with a thump into the bristle
fur of the beaver

and the beaver let out a cry

and bit flippy hard with the serrated buck of
his teeth

but with a wild frenzy of stabs the frog forged
ahead with his work

and soon all gushing in spouts the blood flew

down onto the cold ground they fell and rolled
and bucky bit again

but his thrashing defense faltered under
flippy's relentless jabbing

and the beaver's next bite resulted in a hideous
coughing of red

then moments later his bulky frame shuddered
and there

at last

he fell dead

in the woodsy stretch of woods

down by the misty brook

flippy stood up

out of breath

checked his shiny wounds

and smiled

he would be okay

and sleep soundly to wake

on a bright spring day

so through the leaveless haunted trees he
hopped himself homeward

the light of the moon dimmed to black by the
passing of more clouds

then magically the dark air started to sparkle
with flurries

which drifted in delicate cascading wisps

as a light breeze caused the landscape to shiver
with a wintry rustle

filled with the ghostly echoes of sleigh bells
and icicle chimes

a season in which an amphibian is never awake
to enjoy

the great shifting had come

from brisk to teeth chatter

to downright cold

harvest time had wound down

and hibernation was beckoning

at least to those still breathing to hear the call

like flippy

and on he rushed home

arriving with just enough time to dress his
injuries and crawl into bed

as the flurries grew into real snow that
brightened the cooling carcasses

of all those creatures who had died

during the day

it was marvelous

there was a great new austere silence that
spread

from roots to treetops and into the subzero air
beyond

it felt as peaceful and weightless as childhood

in that woodsy stretch of woods

down by the misty brook

the wind

last night the wind was angry

so it pushed down the old fence

pressed and bullied it into the weeds

while i held onto my black hat by the brim

leaves swirling up like hungry insects

sticking to my coat, biting my neck and hissing

and it felt like snow

the autumn always passes so quickly

and winter sends out its flying thieves

who, with quick transparent hands

strip the red from the trees

and the orange gone now, too

the yellow left in dirty wet patches around

lampposts

a quick death to the glorious fall

last night it became clear

warmth was soon going to be a hard thing to
find

about the author

Bob Stevens is a former party store manager, current librarian and native Michigander. This is the second book in a planned collection of thirteen.

jrefund books (the first eight)

01 dark tales of the inland seas region (2019)

02 dark poems of the inland seas region (2020)

03 dark poems of elsewhere (2021)

04 dark tales of elsewhere (2022)

05 devil in the pines (2023)

06 the last island almanac (2024)

07 the last academic library (2025)

08 the last inland seas unraveling (2026)